Pit Pat

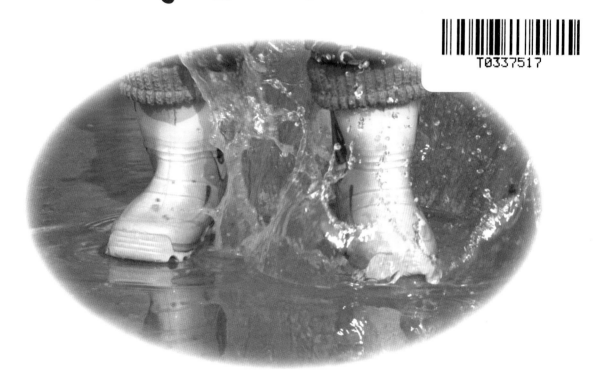

Written by Charlotte Raby

Collins

pit pat

pit pat

tip tap

tip tap

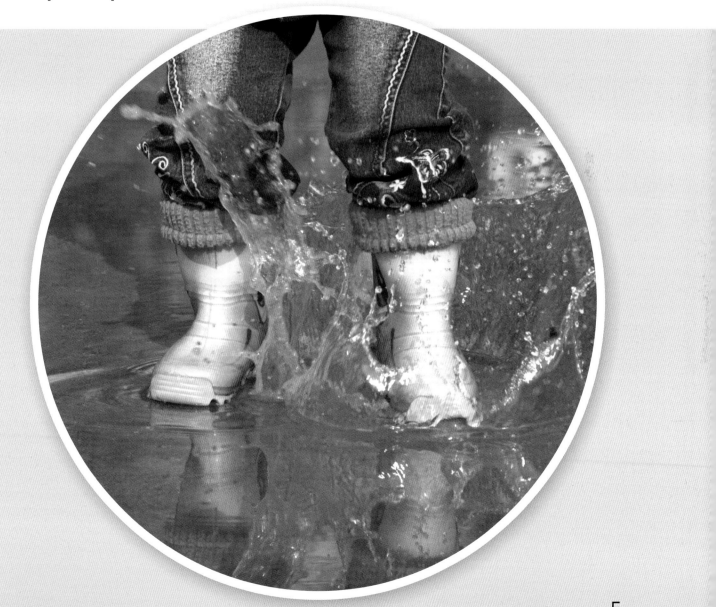

pit pat

tip tap

7

pit pat

pit pat

tip tap it

pat pat it

sip sip

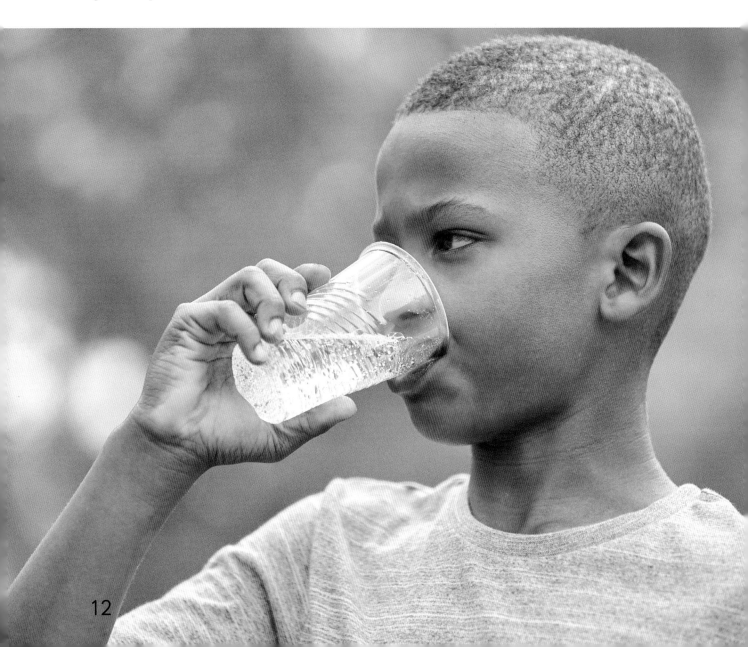

nap nap

/a/

 After reading

Letters and Sounds: Phase 2

Word count: 26

Focus phonemes: /s/ /a/ /t/ /p/ /i/ /n/

Curriculum links: Understanding the World: The World

Early learning goals: Listening and attention: listen to stories, accurately anticipating key events and respond to what is heard with relevant comments, questions or actions; Understanding: answer 'how' and 'why' questions about experiences and in response to stories or events; Reading: children use phonic knowledge to decode regular words and read them aloud accurately

Developing fluency

- Your child may enjoy hearing you read the story. Alternatively, you could take turns to read a page.
- Encourage your child to use actions to act out each of the words in the story.

Phonic practice

- Point to the word **pat** on page 2. Model sounding it out p/a/t and blending the sounds together **pat**.
- Ask your child to do the same with the word **tap** on page 4. Point out the 'a' sound in both words.
- Now look at 'I spy sounds' on pages 14 and 15 together. Which words can your child find in the picture with the 'a' sound in them? (apples, dad, mat, tablet, bag, lap)

Extending vocabulary

- Ask your child if they can think of any other words that describe what it sounds like when it is raining. (e.g. pitter patter, splash)
- Ask your child what words they would use to describe thunder and lightning. (e.g. loud, powerful, bright)